Celebrating Differences

We All Have Different Abilities

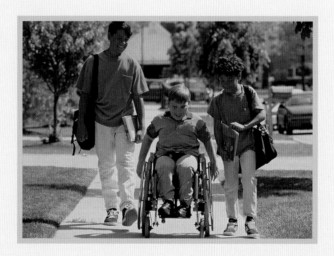

by Melissa Higgins

Raintree is an imprint of Capstone Global Library Limited, a company incorporated in England and Wales having its
registered office at 264 Banbury Road, Oxford, OX2 7DY – Registered company number: 6695582

www.raintree.co.uk
myorders@raintree.co.uk

Text © Capstone Global Library Limited 2016
The moral rights of the proprietor have been asserted.

Jeni Wittrock, editor; Gene Bentdahl, designer; Svetlana Zhurkin, media researcher;
Kathy McColley, production specialist; Marcy Morin, studio scheduler; Sarah Schuette, photo stylist

ISBN 978 1 4747 2361 9 (hardback)
20 19 18 17 16
10 9 8 7 6 5 4 3 2 1

ISBN 978 1 4747 2365 7 (paperback)
21 20 19 18 17
10 9 8 7 6 5 4 3 2 1

British Library Cataloguing in Publication Data
A full catalogue record for this book is available from the British Library.

Acknowledgements
We would like to thank the following for permission to reproduce photographs: Alamy: Photofusion Picture Library, 11,
Stock Connection Distribution, 19; Capstone Studio: Karon Dubke, 7, 9, 13; Corbis: Brian Mitchell, 5, 15, moodboard,
cover; Getty Images: Don Smetzer, 1; iStockphoto: Christopher Futcher, 17, fatihhoca, 20–21.

We would like to thank Gail Saunders Smith, PhD and Donna Barkman, Children's Literature Specialist and Diversity
Consultantant Ossining, New York for their invaluable help in the preparation of this book.

Every effort has been made to contact copyright holders of material reproduced in this book. Any omissions will be
rectified in subsequent printings if notice is given to the publisher.

All the internet addresses (URLs) given in this book were valid at the time of going to press. However, due to the
dynamic nature of the internet, some addresses may have changed, or sites may have changed or ceased to exist since
publication. While the author and publisher regret any inconvenience this may cause readers, no responsibility for any
such changes can be accepted by either the author or the publisher.

Note to parents and teachers

This book describes and illustrates different abilities. The images support early readers in
understanding the text. The repetition of words and phrases helps early readers to learn new
words. This book also introduces early readers to subject-specific vocabulary words, which are
defined in the Glossary. Early readers may need assistance to read some words and to use the
Contents, Glossary, Read more and Index sections of the book.

Made in China

Contents

On my own

I can do things on my own.

At school and at home,

I am busy, busy, busy.

I can get ready

It's morning. I put on my

T-shirt and pull up my socks.

Head to toe, I do it

all by myself.

When I make my own
breakfast, I don't spill a drop.
I'm proud of what I can do.

It's time for school! I can't wait
to see my friends on the bus.

I can learn

My teacher asks a question.

I know the answer.

Pick me, teacher!

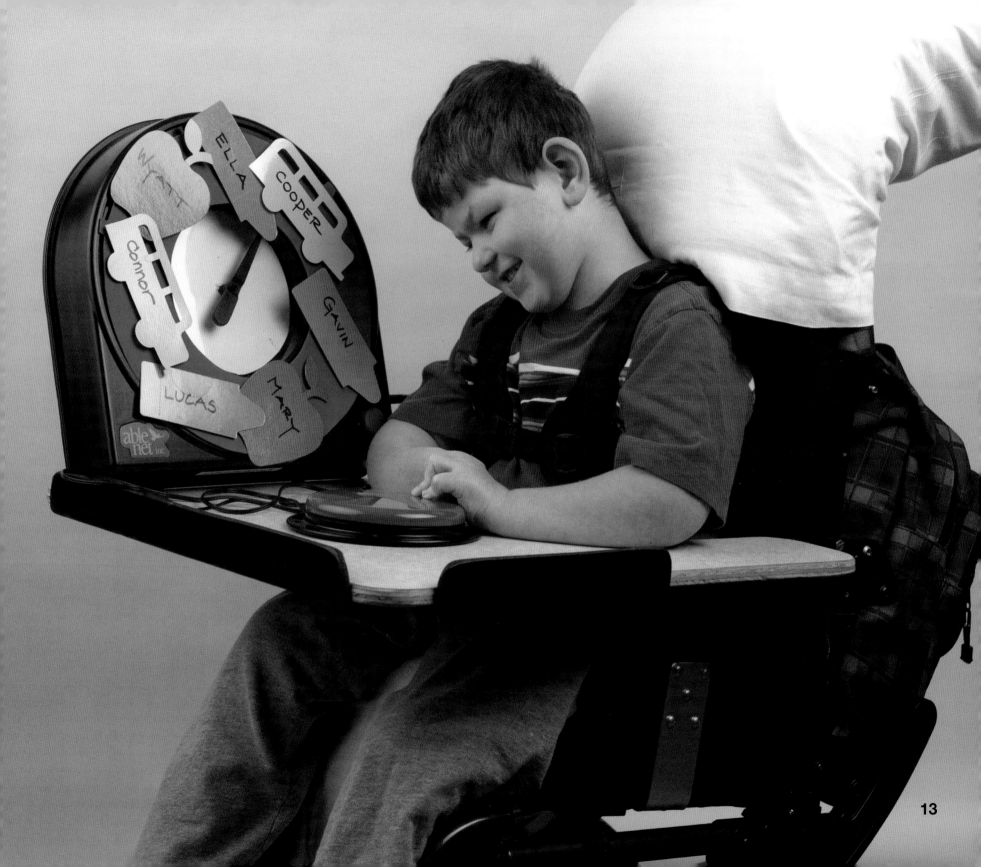

Numbers are fun. I am good
at maths. I help my friend with
a tricky problem.

I can play

Here comes the ball.

THWAP!

I catch it in my stick.

Do you want to join our game?

The swings are crowded today.

I wait for my turn.

WHOOSH!

It is worth the wait!

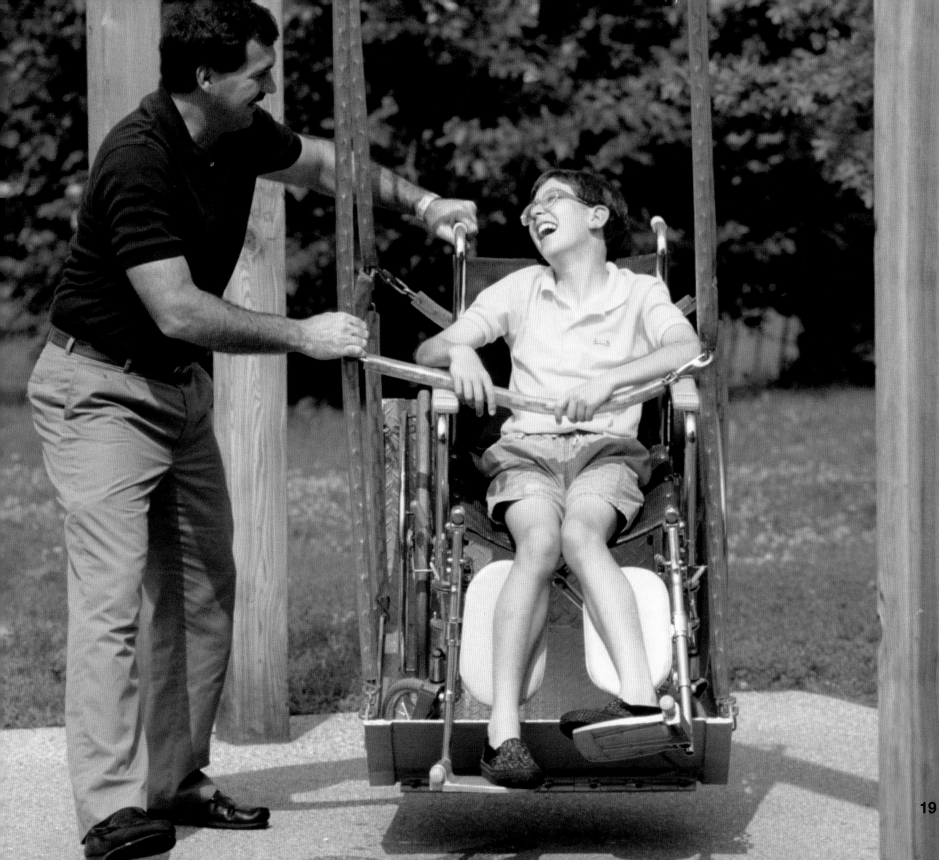

Let's have some fun!

We sing, clap and

play songs. There are

so many things we can do.

What can you do?

Glossary

crowded lots of people

proud feeling good about who you are and what you do

Read more

I Can Take Turns (Me and My Friends), Daniel Nunn (Raintree, 2014)

I Know Someone with Down's Syndrome (Understanding Health Issues), Vic Parker (Raintree, 2012)

Laura and Silky (City Farm), Jessie Williams (Curious Fox, 2013)

Proud (Dealing with Feeling...), Isabel Thomas (Raintree, 2014)

We Are All Different, Rebecca Rissman (Raintree, 2011)

What I Like About Me! A Book Celebrating Differences, Allia Zobel-Nolan (Reader's Digest Children's Books, 2005)

Index